PRIMATE POEMS

DANNY ROSEN

LITHIC PRESS
FRUITA, COLORADO

Design & layout by Kyle Harvey

PRIMATE POEMS
Danny Rosen
ISBN 978-0-9975017-0-4
Lithic Press

LITHIC PRESS
fine books for an old planet

www.lithicpress.com

for my dad, Jay Rosen, tikkun olam,
poet of the family, and so much more

Yet stones have stood for a thousand years, and pained thoughts
   found
The honey of peace in old poems.

–Robinson Jeffers

CONTENTS

ONE

TWO

PRIMATE POEMS

ONE

WHO WOULD CHANGE THE WORLD

Only blue
behind a swollen orange moon
dropping western before dawn,
and stars seen from the bottom
where teeming I lay thinking,
in a cattail field invading,
standing tall and drinking
in the morning ever filling
from a very old well.

Walking through
the wetland in a distant early dew,
came a warning from a great owl,
in a tree hit by lightning,
of a certain aging raven
who would have changed the world—
if he wasn't busy cawing
swooping black in a fit marauding,
flying onyx to the morning,
forgetting one and all. Still,

morning's mirror shudders
with a sudden recognition
of the face looking in it—
as it begins to disappear, thinning
like the far horizon, the body always ending,
the moon's orange falling, the dawn
ever growing, in the mist,
in the blue so near.

FTL

Reader became the seer.
Seer turned to stone.
Stone sat still.
Stillness burned.
Burn knew no bound.

No atom. No quantum.
No mind, but imagination—
which is faster than the speed of light.

TRILOBITE JESUS

He did not die for my sins,
but from a sudden build-up of ash,
a thickening weight.

The newest level of the sea found him
awash on a hardened beach, by a river,
burrowed in, covered over, fast asleep
in far Utah, sending out one last signal.
The mud lithified about his lobe, all
his work turned to stone, he lost hold
of every belief. Trilobite Jesus,

He didn't die for my sins,
                    but He came back,
and I am drilling a hole in His head
with a carbide hammer-drill bit,
                    to make of Him a pendant
to hang from 'round my neck; an albatross
to mark this moment, this moment on the cross.

NOT LIKE THAT

Not like that time the mushroom beach tilted
and the catalog boys walked off a ripped page
asking, what time is it? how much farther is it?
where are we? and we fell down into the trees
bending, laughing low, no, not like that, but
it was a tilting, and walking was difficult.

Not like that liner you smacked over second
and everything stopped: the wind, the sound
in the stands, all the hands that fell away.
I only sensed you rounding the bases,
but knew you'd be safe at home. No,
not like that, but that smack rang true
just like that tooth I lost in deep left.

Not like that science classroom
with 25 cracked mirrors clinging to the sink
just to stay afloat. Nope, not like that!

It came cracking through electric windows
like lightning, like fire, like *Light My Fire*
in the back seat of the '64 Rambler,
Dad's fingers on the dial with news
of a rendezvous out in space.
Like that guy in tight black pants
at the New York World's Fair,
like that first bellbottom blue,
like the first time I met you
on the side of that rock tower,
twisting like a devil, hanging
at the end of a very thin line. More

like the first time I stood facing the wall
in the back of the 2nd grade classroom
laughing with Steve Lawrence,
laughing and laughing and trying
to keep from crying, finally knowing
the losing battle.

THE STRANGER

Back in the day, when you couldn't tell if the sky was falling
or was it just another piece of the goddamned ceiling,
we drank shots in the basement with the stranger,
then drove into the city and left him on the corner,
where glowing wires twisted lines that crowded
in so we could hardly breathe.

The planet turned a cheek, went along with all the spin.

We spun on mustang bikes with baseball cards
clipped in the spokes, into far precincts always
warned against, where else to sit and drink
those stolen beers? At least we had that pedaling.
Back doors had our ears. Shadows cracked
in the slightest gaps, flags menaced
only at half staff and by God
you took off your hat
for the supper shake, no-one could fake
a cherry pie, why don't we just take a drive?
Officer Clem was no child's friend,
and Mr. Commissioner was utterly straight,
hard-headed and very lucky—
that time I beaned him square from left field.
You, in the stands, cheering as I struck out again,
sitting quiet when I doubled down the line.
No one questioned the brown bag at your feet.
The heat was just the Sun.
                    And when the Dam broke
everyone was shocked:
those in the small houses, those in the big houses,
those in the houses that floated down the valley
just held on tight, blaming no-one.
In an attic window...

bobbing up and down, dazed and looking out,
photographed and framed, edge-blurred and grim...
the stranger, who one day pushed open the doors
and bought one for the house, no questions asked.
Just like the country in those days, we drank our shots
and ate the glass.

ON A GREEK HILL

Stooped in black on a garden slope,
wrapped in a tight-lipped century.
On Hydra's hip a white-rock road,
on a Greek hill above the sea.
No talk she snapped with disdain,
grabbed at her gray mane,
tightened a band about her head,
yelled across the dying field
to the animals by the broken well.
                              The killings

all too well remembered. How she
looked at me, what she did not say,
what the neighbors heard. How she
lit the torch, sharply turned, went away.

HARRISON ODJEGBA OKENE, WRECK SURVIVOR

ABUJA, 28 May, 2013 (Reuters) — Twelve crew
members are missing after the tug, Jascon-4, capsized
in rough seas off the coast of Nigeria...

It was dark, man. It was dark, and cold. Three days
in the water, all alone. I had one bottle of coke. One
of the twelve who went down with the boat, I lived
upside down at the bottom of the sea. It was dark, man,
when I saw the light, coming closer, closer, and going away.
I grabbed at that diver, reached for his foot...he was so afraid,
as if he'd seen a ghost. He's alive! alive! alive! that diver yelled
to the surface searchers, up there, looking for corpses.

That diver gave me water and watched as I drank, to see
was I a man or some phantom of the deep. Or was I a chink
in the armor of how we sometimes think when alone in the dark
and oh so cold, at the bottom of the sea with nowhere to go?

LOCAL POLITICS

I turn away from those who know
what is right, no matter how
right they are. Or left.

WHAT DO YOU DO?

Beavers move upstream each fall and chew
through winter on the elms.
At dusk I see them by their dam,
emerging from a wet day,
holding sticks they must chew.
Rising to leave for community's sake,
into their pond I throw a rock, yup,
that's what I do. Nights,
I hear slapping in the dark. Mornings,
I find their work, what's left behind:
de-barked branches sharpened to spears,
bent-down cattails leading to rising water,
piles of wood chips with tooth marks.
Overactive all night long, serious and slow,
come April, the beavers go downstream
for the summer to raise their young
by the river, where they chew, and chortle
at those who ask, what do you do?

MAKING FIRE

Cullen arrived before the day
with his yucca stalk,
cottonwood root, and cedar fluff
that we blew into flame.
Under a green tree we looked at the gray sky,
talked about not much, sat until it was time to go,
then we got up and went
at the start of the shortest day.
Day broke
and we took our arrows out.

Warm with meat, Cullen
squatted by the fire, on a bluff near the river,
iced over in midwinter, no gloves, no coat,
like the wooly men of colder times…
standing still on their cave slopes,
looking silent for long spells,
gripping sticks ground to spears,
running with dogs beside the beast,
screaming, stabbing, dodging tusk,
taunting with a sap torch,
urging the herd toward a rock drop-off.

Just before dark I saw
Cullen twist his spear into the soft
at the top of the chest,
just below the trunk-head.
He stood his ground, thinking
to stand his ground, and to thrust it in.
Beast and man, reeling, running away
watching death descend, making fire
by the river's bend, under Orion's frozen sky,
rubbing his hands, Cullen thinks of warmer times.

ALL OUR FATHERS

Wasn't our fault all the homes were closed, locked and barred,
or that the churches went door to door,
or that the revelers had such sad eyes—
their message of peace the smallest font,
or that wanting out of the war zone was all the pilgrim's sought.

Wasn't our fault the onslaught of returned gifts began
with diamonds no longer holding the heart, but the gun,
and everyone sunk to having fun, on the very day the graves were found.

Wasn't our fault the youngest son bought the farm so young.
He clutched, fell back, dropped like a stone, over and over and over again
he died so real, better than the TV dead, shot in the back on the front yard hill.
What tough children we were, living with the bullseye on the town square,
where the railroad screamed and the donkey said,
'all our fathers were hunters, kid.'

LONG-SPINED THORNY OYSTER

(a shell from Mom)

Your red splashed umbo
and lines of delicate spines
are too fragile to touch, but
must be held. God-hinged,

serrated tight, sun-burst
on white, pink-edged inside.
You opened to feed but
shutting down was your strength.

Spondylidae spondylidae,
pearlescent home you made
for me. Mother of mud,
chrysanthemum of the sea.

With no weight now you lie
finished, unafraid, you remain
an unhinged shell, half-buried
in a potted plant in my sun room.

AT THE CHILDREN'S RECITAL

Small life forms prance young before old
life forms sitting straight in straight rows.
Chocolate medallion melts on my tongue,
bunny-masked minis loom large on the wall,
flashing lights accelerate tutu-clad tip toe,
tip toe, tip toe, jump over and roll, roll, roll,
and applause. The children line along the wall
and somehow, learn to live inside their bodies.
A purple sass shows some leg and does the crab.
Parents, friends, brothers, sisters, aunts and uncles,
everyone expects to live forever.

The children are innocent, yearning and lovely.
Long may the supermarkets of my land be free
from the empty chaos of the natural world.

BEHOLDEN

Those who are beholden to no one
are so strong, almost
like stone.

IMAGINE THAT!

There are no straight lines in nature.
There are many straight lines in nature.

for Buff Orpington

A DAY LIKE TODAY

Sitting on the dock with Kyle
reading Stevens with blackbirds, talking
the positive and negative of everything,
questioning the academy, the two sides,
in and out of nodding off, looking across
the drainage, wider than usual this spring—
winter's beaver work not yet washed out,
I see water fall over the small dam,
as if a great chasm lay before me.

The willows are greening, my socks are off.
The sun is hot.
I read The Snow Man.
Kyle reads Thirteen Ways.
Icicles hang in the cloudless sky,
in the cloud-filled mind, we are flawed.

I never wrote to Mister Jim
who lived downstream,
before he went to old Mexico.
                              No owl
in the owl box. A few early butterflies.
Winter's leftover woodpile.

I walk up to the house to retrieve
Jim's book on the counter...along
the pallet walk, up the wood chip path,
through the metal gate, past dogs who wait,
into the yard I walk—when something funny
occurs and I fall over, done, gone.

TWO

EXSCIND: TO CUT OUT OR OFF

from, *A.Word.A.Day with Anu Garg*

Skei is the root,
said the father to the son
as the bone split under the stone.
Exscindere, the man hummed

to himself as the boy worked and sounds
like years of aches in the back and lines
of the long leaf, and the long bloom

he can still taste ...exscindere... the dry fall,
the rebirth, the ghost at the end (exscindere
exscindere) will heal no further.
Skei! screamed the son to the father.

WATCHING BASEBALL

'…imaginary gardens with real toads in them…'
– Marianne Moore

Watching baseball…
with contempt for it, its simple contrivances,
the way it's designed for another commercial break
every half-inning, the control freak agents, managers and players
constant rancor at the umpires, the ceaseless announcers—
like house flies when the cows are close, all the scores
from around the league, contempt for the season's length,
the whole country caught up in the Thing. The thing:
like watching paint dry, say those who describe It as,
dull inaction of half-athletes—whose exploits are always
about average.

And yet, growing up with it, one finds between the lines
in Baseball, something genuine: the old man and a cigar,
history, strategy, order, symmetry, 'ladies and gentlemen,
please rise and sing along…' stretch, have a dog and a beer,
spill your pop going for a foul, stand up and yell out loud
at the damned bums, and give praise

to the natural human animal in action—
hale young bipeds performing at their peak, grown men
in uniform, ready and willing to run through walls,
spending the energy of any young warrior, with no killing,
usually no blood.

Tonight, the guy pitching is the pitcher who threw a pitch
behind the head of the batter at the plate—six years ago:
big brouhaha, the benches cleared, a punch was thrown,
couple of ejections. In the booth, in the stands, in hanky-
waving rabid fans, anticipation settles over the field
where no love is lost and there could be a fight!

The world is not perfect, but a 5-4-3 double play
is a beautiful thing to see. The image at once held
forever in the mind, conjured up at abrupt times,
times that defy time—like a humpback line drive…

The Pitcher
goes into his wind-up, looks the runners back, lifts,
twists, pauses on one leg, stretches back, exhales big,
uncorks at once. His arm bends (on the tube in slo-mo)
sickeningly back, as if to snap. He throws a curve.

The Batter
speaks with his bat, adjusts his nuts so nonchalant, spits,
rubs on the tar, crosses himself up to God, wraps the straps
of his gloves tight, digs in, takes a few swings, looks up: sees…

the trajectory of a white ball arc out into the black night.

He bangs his bat on the plate, two on, one out,
top of the ninth, down a run. He takes his stance
(radio dreams of kids in bed half asleep across the land)
The brute grips and tenses, breathes and releases,
whips his club around, grabs his woman by the hair,
lines one down the third base line.

The Third Baseman
is ambushed by that shot, the stalwart at the hot corner
can only react, knowing vet he is, he lunges, snags, leaps
to his feet throwing and around the horn they go:
third to second to first. Game over!
The announcer grabs his heart leapt out his mouth,
stuffs it back down, continues to talk.
The hawkers of beer fold up their carts.
The drunks stumble off to other fights.
A blind man in the stands, stands, can almost see
the old home team run off the field so diamond green.

THE BISHOP

The Bishop railed against the homo lovers,
held seminars to cure the gay-afflicted.

At the Covenant Ceremony, Bishop got busted,
traveling with his hand-picked boys:
exclusive gems, spiritual sons, long-fellow-youths.
He gave them jewels, exchanged vows,
removed his belt, put the candle out,
shot up in the back, and lured them
to his Bentley in the drive.
He promised to keep them from harm.

Shaking his golden bangles he cried,
'Jesus was not a poor man.'
Pastor of a loaded congregation,
an international corporation, 'not just a bunch
of bumbling preachers…I deny these ugly charges…'
said the man who knew what his flock wanted
as he sent his boys down the broken path,
searching for that one clean birth.

THE GRAFT

In the Temple of the Scoundrel
on a dais hewn from rock, a prime damsel
at her peak, pierced by a hulk (from behind)
screamed and joined the scion to the stock.

Ceremony of a certain Moon,
greased-up bodies in a grease-lit lair.
The farmers all performed the graft—
feral mustang unto twisted mare.

Saplings from two trees made a new tree,
a grown thing, grown by those known
to make stuff, and go a little lunatic
out on the portico—

the Man of Tears rose to say, 'They are idolaters,
we will have nothing to do with their opinions,
their abominations, their lewd displays.
And we must guard against the graft...'

but the Moon continued to gain its height,
the vamps continued to show their concern,
tempting the shepherds and believers alike,
to take them down by the trees that burn.

COLD BORDEAUX

I'm looking for a church.
It is impossible to find.
The city is a grand theatre
in a cold river wind.
I take the bus. I hop the tram.
People are talking. I marvel at all
I do not understand.

Fossil shells in church walls
merge with the fears of man, paintings
of the Savior can not help but fade
behind the barricade, lies
the landscape of the Lord.

In the Cathedral of Saint Andre
I sit with ghosts, I know them well,
they're in my blood, we're bastards all.

Ms. Felicity lays a hand on my knee I know
it's a lie. Oh lord, I just don't know
all these things I think I know.

Schoolboy crosses the father, son,
and holy ghost, raises his brow,
flips his nose, shivs his pal, asks le Père,
how much did this place cost?

Cracked statues dance angelic
under darkened white-rock domes,
organ thunder thunders
over children on old benches
on their way away from home.

Below high ogeed arches,
something strikes down in the bone.

MANDELBROT

What shape is a mountain?
Can we build a coastline here?
Why does the river go there?

Mandelbrot worked with questions
and thoughts often reserved for kids
and poets. Simple is simple and life is
not fair.

He moved a lot and learned to keep
moving, he saw things move
differently: plane and simple, complex,
fractured.

He knew what it meant to flee, knew
the weight of family. His uncle lead him
to a zoo inside his head. He chased

those animals into fractals, his mind
a hotness, his life devoted to the edge
of roughness.

THAT RUSSIAN METEORITE

aio Vano!

From dashboard cams on Russian roads,
the scatter fields and sonic booms,
the scientists divined the path
of the star-like rock as it neared the earth.

We spoke of that
as she swept the debris,
kneeling down on swelling knees,
picking up every last goddamned piece

of the goblet she smashed
against the cottonwood tree. Ai!
Her love rises like shooting stars flash. "Ai!"
she said, "it felt so fucking good to smash that glass!"

THREE BOYS ON A CLIFF

Three boys on a cliff (in an old photograph)
above an ancient inland sea. Wrapped in black
and white towels, and quite astonished, they sing:

> "The cliffs were once the sea,
> The cliffs were once the sea—
> filled with now and living things."

Hugging his knees (a living now) one boy
looks high, stands to salute the limestone sky,
turns, dives, swims into a sea long dry.

BANG BANG

Outside the planetarium little Joseph stood
next to a pigtailed girl with thick glasses.
"What made the big bang, bang?" Joseph asked.
Bang bang, I thought, before I could say anything,
Joseph said, "I think two molecules of nothing,
raw nothing and regular nothing,
came together and caused the big bang to bang."
Then the little blonde girl,
standing at the center of the expanding universe,
stuck her fingers into her mouth, pulled her lips apart
and said, "Thee? I jutht lotht my latht tooth."

ECLIPSED

Enlightenment I do not want.
A rock is a rock, a toad a toad,
I am happy to know, and not know.
The day is a road. The sky is at set.
The moon turns an earthly red—

tranquility bleeds on the broken heart-
shaped rock, hung behind dead sunflowers
                    nailed to the shed door.
The moon hangs by the pitchfork.
I have been a fool for love.

THE RED DEER CAVE BOY

One afternoon, an early Modern Man raped a Denisovan girl
in the province known as Yunan. The day after the ice cliff
began to melt, her boy went to play in the Red Deer Cave.

Falling rock covered the child over. That mother looked
everywhere, went insane, forgot to eat, forgot to breathe,
got lost in that ancient air. She wrung her roses,

sang to the moon, sat fast, not too soon, not too slow,
sang to the roses, sang to the roundness rung about
in darkness, sang songs of solar epochs, sung with no sound.

After twelve thousand years her son was found
by another boy gone to play in the Red Deer Cave.
He found the head of that dead runaway, took it home,
set it on the shelf in his Chinese bedroom.

SUPPERTIME ON THE LITTLE KNIFE ANTICLINE

"Well, fellas…," said the one known as McGee,
to the grime-covered greasers gathered about him
in the doghouse, standing dim in the half light
and thunder of the rig they no longer heard at all,
nor the clang of the string at the derrick top, so high
over the lonely Earth, the hours turn to the right so slow,
like the Moon all night all day all night again, hanging
over the tumult of that precious hole.

And the Moon hung over a white Dodge Ram
kicking up the thirsty road,
heading fast for Dickinson, taking Harald,
the new hand - who lost three fingers to the chain.
McGee found one just after they left, rinsed it off,
set it on the manifold, plucked the nail, flicked it away,
peeled the skin slowly back, held it on a paper plate,
sprinkled salt, looked up and said, "who's hungry?"

THE STORY OF A DOG

with little to do
I continue
to do

little

like a dog
with failing hips
I walk about on all fours
cough
bark at passing cars
sleep most of the time

everyday
I wake
stretch
and bow down
for a head scratch
for a small treat

I bow down
to the opposable thumb
to the pen in hand
to what is written now
the story of a dog

THE MOUNTAINS OF JAPAN

This morning I woke
in the mountains of Japan,
even though I've never been
          to the mountains of Japan
or anywhere else in that radiant land.

This morning the angle of reeds
tilting oriental struck right to this east
where I reside with the rising sun,
portrayed as a red round,
waving a rose on a white background.

This morning I heard a Japanese aeroplane,
buzzing along in the Asian sky, angling down
to paddy fields, hidden by low-lying clouds,
lost in a mist—that would be here just now,
over this small desert town,
if it wasn't such a blue and cloudless day,
and if Japan was not so far away.

STICK OUT YOUR CAN, HERE COMES THE GARBAGE MAN

"Lot of pussy on this job," said my new boss Bob,
as he pulled the traditional rear-loader down a tight alley
past rows of full dumpsters. A gaunt woman pushed
open the door behind the bakery. Aping her, grabbing his
groin, grinning at me, hooking the bin, Bob asked,
"wanna see my gun?" He backed up that alley ever so slowly,
past the baker leaning against the screen door, finally
out of earshot, Bob yelled at her out his window,
(while turning through a yellow)
        "You can sit on my face!" honk, honk.

Racing to the next job, happy Bob, doing Elvis,
        "You can do anything you want,
        just don't step on my blue suede
        uh-huh, uh-huh."

I ran into Bob's glory one inglorious morning...
"Gotta start early," he'd said, "be at my house at 4."
That north Philadelphia morning I pounded his cold door.
"Changed my mind," said Sleepy Bob, standing in pajamas,
rubbing his belly, "let's start at 6:30. If you don't touch Glory,
you can sleep on the couch in the basement,
you touch her, I'll kill you."

That day Bob had a headache, I offered a joint
he did not want. I offered a lead pipe, he lifted,
let out a beef grunt, and drove twice more
todadump todadump todadump, dump, dump.
Two more flat tires, goddamnedfuckingflattires.

Driving home late
through Manayunk's haze, its river street scenes,
brick on brick, row on row, three-stories and a stoop
blaring Philly radios, smoke pouring out the windows,
blown-out in Roxborough. Sun going down a dirty road,
disappearing way out west.

SOMETHING LIKE A LIGHT PATH

The universe turned to look before the bullet struck
at what lay here—not why—not nothing—not
now—naught but another day of the universe
being itself, learning a little something
like a light path, a light path, it was

just another day, the slug went in, thought
struck but of course thought is fast   time
slowed. The universe did not mind leaving
this mode, two-legged and sexy as it is,
frontal lobe of the sky, picture that,
cloud that you are, sturm und alle!

Dammitall! The universe will miss itself
but forget   quick   as the weight of the spark,
the wakened zip—evaporates—the bullet penetrates
meat thought mind sky, cloud hole wide big and in,
in, in again, out again, Finnegan had a wake, too.

THREE

'51 MICKEY MANTLE

for Heinz, in Philly, 1968

He told me he was going to Vietnam
and beat me up out on the field all day long
I worshipped him, and learned to look
so close for the lost balls from home runs

hit into the woods, with his words
on the wind, "I'll kick your ass
if I come up there and find that ball."
That story in the Evening Bulletin:

a baseball card show at the Sheraton,
news of a card auction. That box of cards
he gave to me—with stories of the infantry,
"well, you know, I might not be coming back."

Like a time bomb in the closet's dark…
a '51 Mickey Mantle in excellent shape - no shit!
I quit my job, paid off the truck, headed west.
He returned. I've never been back.

THE THISTLE PULLER

The bare-handed thistle puller stood.
The young amerikaner approached.
Nephew or cousin? They greeted each other
for the first time ever, exchanged pidgin
pleasantries for a minute and a half,
before the thistle called the puller
back to work, to what he knows…this valley
and its hills, far as the eye can see, he knows

to bend at the waist and a little at the knee
to keep on pulling he daydreams: what waits at home,
the two paths he takes each day, the one road that goes
to town, that one he's never been down, he knows
enough of that town. He reads nights and knows
of that which he does not know. He does not know
what lies ahead, but what's to do right now,
and when he gets there, there he is

pulling seven times his weight today,
loading the truck he got in 1958, leading
the well meaning foreigner whose bleeding hands
drip on the ground of these war-torn lands.

1974 STANLEY CUP CHAMPIONS

What was not there five minutes ago
is what I now step right into. Oh shit,
that bastard dog, the one most self-absorbed,
laid another turd just by the back door.

I shoulder the shovel and walk the yard.
The dogs follow. I look into the tall grass.
The dogs look away at nothing fast, or watch me,
but not real close. The dogs pause when I pause.
They are above this work.
I scoop their crap into the broad flat blade
of the shovel, and turn to take a wrist shot
over the fence into the cattails.

Or, I go for a quick backhand, shooting
for the corner of the net, like Dornhoefer in '74,
when the Flyers played for the Cup in overtime,
that announcer cried, "he shoots, he SCORES!"
I made mash-ups late on school nights,
on a recorder in the room at the top of the stairs...
"Barber dumps it up the wing, Clarke gets it in front,
he turns, he shoots, he SCORES!" (He grins
his toothless grin, always takes one for the team)
"Ashbee goes down to his knees, lays down on the ice,
his head bleeds... MacLeish grabs the rebound,
spins, shoots, he SCORES!" I hear the turds plop

against the pond's far shore. The sound of that word, plop,
makes me laugh out loud—as I triumphantly turn and wave
to the crowd—of three dogs sitting still—no cheers,
no thanks, no thrill; they have no fear of shit rolling downhill.

KEITH AND KATHY

Keith and Kathy married at the Greek cafe.
He came for coffee. Her shift was early.
They kissed quick before he left for the DMV.

They had two kids, lots of friends, weekends off,
softball games, tubes in the river, life in the 'burbs,
hot tub out back, pizza and beer; 26 good years.

A quick sick led to Keith's death, and his last scheme
at the graveside: a 21-tab salute, with 21 cans of Genesee,
his kind of prayer for his friends kind of peace.

THE BEAVER AND ITS WORK

The blind woman caressed the cottonwood stump
that had been beaver cut in late winter's warming cold.

She fingered the silver wood, weather-soft and smooth,
swayed to and fro at a vision of their chomp and pull.

I spoke of the beaver tooth, little that I could, she felt
crescentic bits of wood piled where the tree once stood.

They cut the tree to hauling lengths and drag their loads
down to the stream. She dreamed the beaver's boggy roads,

saw them build beneath the day, saw dry land become a pond,
and walking on the wood chip path, her hands found

the chewed ends, she scanned again their pointed sharps,
her face was rapt. The blind woman looked keenly up,

she saw the beaver, all its work, the helpless plight
of lovers everywhere, and some sense of a bigger bite.

NOETHER'S THEOREM

The laughing mathematician let her hair down hither.
Emily spoke of the symmetry of conservative things,
and of rings. She defined new fields
and swam with the men in the men's pool.

They loved her so,
but she remained loyal to the precision of numbers,
would not marry, and never spoke of her affairs.

THE STAGE COACH

In the beginning was the rock,
the word, and the man with a jug
beneath the sky with what he heard
by the hearth in his home. He thought

of wisdom and the road, the journey done,
the wrong turn, the way down, the come back,
back to thatch with its wine supply, the mountains
ahead, and all the mountains left behind.

TWO DUCKS

One duck
in the pond.

Another friend
is gone.

MOUNT OLYMPUS

In the boxcar that rounded the bend by the sea,
the man with the pint was thrown from the train.
Confused and blind in a sudden dark and drowned
in his mind, words appeared, not alarmed and not
unlike another time in a dry room with a small dog,
sitting by an unframed oil tacked on the wall...

The dog sat still, fell asleep, shook awake, looked away.
The man looked down the tracks curving on the canvas,
the berm, the bend, and across the sound, Mount Olympus
loomed through clouds that were not even there at all that day.

CARRION

In the south field
I drop creatures that I find
to watch them melt into the ground...

Vulture, dead in the tall grass,
spread-feathered, stinking mess.

Field mouse in the barbecue,
punctured by the jack-dog tooth.

Mule deer, truck-hit,
grotesquerie in the borrow pit.

Muskrat under the wet deck,
head down in the pond muck.

Blackbird who fought a hawk,
cut down by a cold snap.

Bullfrog,
dried out on a rotten log.

And into that mortal realm
a hawk leapt

from a southern elm, tucked
wings and that hawk-eye,

it dove, missed, screeched,
and a human sighed. The hawk

rose, turned all-a-scream,
and began again to dive at me.

THE MEEK TREES

"If a tree falls in the forest and nobody is there to hear it, doesn't it just lie there and rot?"

– Chuck Palahniuk

So sharp so bright across the pond
something broke a sudden end
like the moment life began.

A spiral burn wound down the tree,
a spiral scar I sat beneath,
ascribing some human dignity
to the still standing dead tree:
stern monolith, holy refuge,
mute resurrection.

A most powerful sight I did not see
but glimpsing caught
something like a sound-sight
in the darkest dark of a dark night,
when the wind knocked down the dead tree.
It lies still right where it fell—crushed
the bat box—hell for the hung bat,
but the dead, at last, will give in,
all at once in a forest blowdown,
or a stubborn lone pine.
                    They fall.
                      And, falling
a wave spreads —- over a small space,
it is   at last   a loud
                  whump on the   ground.
No sound
      then,
                no nothing then,
                        nothing but
          the ceaseless consumption
                of those who will inherit

                        the earth

WORLD OF WASTED SEEDS

(for Jack)

The poet on the hill says, there are times
and places a critical mass is reached,
like the Athens of Pericles, in the cafes
of North Beach, or Paris in the 20's.

He mulls the edgeland drop-away
with his mind deep in Pound, he reads aloud
in a proud elder state. He says, I am in a state of,
I'm just not sure...

He for whom the stars call out, reaches for
but does not get, what? I don't know.
I forget. Talk is a river I'm going down.
You get the drink, I'll get the gun,

where have all the siskins gone? Psycho?
Logically, he damns the squirrels,
laments the world of wasted seeds,
longs for the Prague of '68. He fades

with the long wait, the slow cool,
on the hill, under the moon.
He questions the gods,
before shooting them too...

Where are all the soulful creatures?
Where is the poem that has a soul?
What is this compression
that so stimulates this brain?
Mother of God, what does it all mean?

WINTER BIRDS

Fastened to a dead arrival
the pilgrim turned over
twilight of a new century
with a growing belief
in thunder and feeling
stronger than nothing
stranger than gentle
tangled with fertile
words,
shells in stone,
stories born,

bejeweled bones
wrapped in vellum
packed in mud, risen
to the melody of
meadowlark and turtle dove
mourning, mourning the body,
the body of understanding,
understanding despair.
Resist! Surrender.
Interrupt! Stay humble.
Now immortal. Now disturbed.
Now whistling to the winter birds.

KOCH'S GOSHAWK

(for Koch, the neighbor, long dead)

Koch's
goshawk

in his field
in my sight

straight winged
stoned eye

sees the sea
between the sea

on the shore
that is not
to be

divided,
everything is

a shadow
a shape

a rock wall
in a morning mind

sunlight splits
the hawk's eye.

FOSSIL

Scalloped striation not gouged
but pressed in rock, an impressed
shellfish: poor clam, shut down,
sign-post, stone shout, touch me,
I'm dead.

LAID TO REST

The stride of Philitas is a perfect font, walking the length
of the strand, measuring the want of his breath,
sending whistle signals from the island of Cos.

Generally, things became disordered with ether
for the horses (some for me) muses for her,
and poems that saw the sullied empire reeking funereal:
wooden seekers seeking their wasted leaders,
(in hiding from recurring nightmares)
while other lead-shoed walkers, with their fears of flying,
went limping through the streets of Alexander screaming,
'the end is near!'

And the city descended into a dark and ashen day.

Many enjoyed the river beast for their own pleasure,
and treasured the clay soldiers falling.
How the partisans cheered!
No cheer like a freshly severed ear,
like wine glasses smashed on the burning pyre,
like flag-waving fans on the fifty yard line,
like sad stallions leaping from the fire-ships,
swimming to nowhere, free at last.

Thin wind blows over the night, misting what was.
Etna outwaits the palaver with the song of the sod.
A new beam falls gently, lays to rest a risen god.

DOG LOVERS

Such bacchanal and war:
two dogs on the cracked pine floor,

like wild mustangs they leap and kick,
when the hunter Jack spins in for a lick

of the herder on his back—who sighs,
spreads his legs, closes his eyes.

GEOLOGY

for Pop, above Ein Gedi

She sang me into the holy land,
sang to me a haunted song,
sung from a dangling megaphone
hung atop a leaning pole, leaning
over the port and blue blue sea.

Three days from Piraeus gone levantine,
running on Rhodos with the Austrian,
in and out of the gray-haired waves,
reborn in the foam with Keo beer.

Sleeping by a deadened sea,
sucking salt in old Judea, I found myself
five miles north of a walled-in siege,
ambushed by an old cacaphony,
reading into night's holy deep,

Sir Patrick Moore's, *Planets and Stars, a guide,*

bought at Steimatzky's on King David Street
in downtown Tel Aviv, the Spring Mound:
mad with modern sounds, mad with songs
of the not forgotten, mad with wanderers
holding tough to beholden ground, mad
with dancers on midnight tables dancing
with the land, the sky, and an ache to touch
something soft, close, impossible to reach.

Like footsteps on old desert rock, or
waking wet to a broken bell, that and more
amok in my head, and so I walked.

I walked hot, the sun was wide,
cretaceous cliffs cut up the west,
oasis sat just out of sight. I walked up
the rift valley's left side, looked
into a leopard's eye—when it leaped
I saw its big cat stride and thought
of the Austrian's certain hand,
messages spelled in ancient sand,
pulled my eyes down from the sky,
saw my foot right down on earth,
looked across the encrusted sea,
began to think of geology.

OH GOD!

If the possible is quantum
Then god is most wanton

IN THE BEGINNING

for Doc Mears, University of Wyoming

The professor enters the lecture hall silently.
It's the anticipation he loves, the sequence of classes,
row upon row of students, semester on semester,
like the strata beneath his boot, he finds himself
firmly within the infinite.

Gazing up to his new crop, cigar out on the chalk tray,
stub in the pocket of a battered jacket,
slacks stuffed in boots caked in mud that reek
like something called, deep time, I lean forward,

cigar smoke rises past wide ears, close-cropped hair,
glint in his eyes; he sighs and says, "I think it's time to begin."

Geology 101. High school a dim memory…
all those smoky years ago; all those toilets cleaned,
trash collected, lawns mown, tables bussed, nails banged;
all those rock towers climbed with foreign labels:

sandstone? granite? "Geology," the professor says,
"why would anyone want to study geology?" He walks
to the chalkboard, writes in huge capitols, G, E, O, stops,
turns his head back to 100 students, looks right at me,

"because we love the earth and we want to learn
as much about it as we possibly can." Back to the board
he finishes spelling, L, O, G, Y, turns to face his captives
and says, "At least, I hope that's why we study geology."

I see years opening: walking through that breached anticline,
traversing this topographically reversed basaltic ridge,
climbing an aplite dike into the sky, wandering to planets
beyond the sun, learning to travel to distant stars,
getting closer and closer and closer to home.

JOHN GLENN IN A SPACE SUIT

Up the stairs I walk in slow motion
thinking about my atoms, my electrons,
my quantum world, and of words
that do not mean what we think they mean,
or what we thought: that something
so small with such a subtle sound,
can lead to a need to know better
the one long day.
            And I think of deep space: stars, nebula,
'one-small-step,' John Glenn in a space suit,
and that touched Einstein, goofing on a light beam
surfing gravity across the galaxy,
conjuring up a quantum sea, seeing packets
of little dreams…I see them
and my atoms that never slow,
no matter which way up the stairs I go.

OLD MAN ON THE MOUNTAIN

for Jack Mueller

For every man on the mountain
there is an old man on the mountain.

By his home on the mountain the old man
stands in a high Tibetan wind, the atmosphere
is thin, log hill has god below, below the goddess
and the god of snow. On a rim of belligerent stone-
cemented sand, athwart a fast moraine, the old man
shoots the Moon with a .22. "You Bastard Moon! You
you Bastard," he screams, then turns to murder the word:
Awesome! There's a hoard in his head so direct to connect
to anything, anytime, and to nothing, on the mountain
every man encounters nothing, often, late at night,
when the light goes black, the old man goes out,
comes back from the edge to sing, blow his flute,
and seduce his Kathryn—doe-eyed by the window feeder.
He fishes for chipmunks with tied walnuts, fucks with people,
and watches over the planet from 22,000 miles. He smiles
on the mountain immersed in nothing. The old man
always comes back with a little something up his sleeve,
a little something to give the young man on the mountain.

FOUR

EROSION OF THE ANCESTRAL ROCKIES

Gravel and sand laid down on a broad flood plain,
piled muck, thick and thin, marsh and dune, humid-lush,
low-land-like long-ago-Georgia: coal in the western swamp!

Laramide Orogen: a slow mountain-building event.
A slow crushing dislocation—as when any life is shaken
up go mountains, down fall boulders, our ancestors
with no footwear, ran along a sinking shore, ran on soft
marine mud, ran past dying turtles and a mass fish death:

the deposit a squirm, a while, a settled down, a covered over
by hot black rock, frozen and left behind, harder than
the lapping stone, a black snake ridge in the desert
west of Farmington. Uplift, erosion, long time
and us—spilling out our earthen guts.

ON THE BEACH WITH MAIMONIDES

while reading his, Guide for the Perplexed

By an old channel last night on the beach with Maimonides
I sat smoking cigarettes with my fingers digging in the sand
in the land of imagination we commiserated on our meeting
and the reality of us eating bread and olives
while sitting on this beach.

The son of Maimon spit a pit into the sea and said,
I swear that I have been dead for seven hundred years,
but these tears are wet, this face is flesh, and I fear
your corporeal sense has such a solid weight. And fate?
It goes not as you want. He bit into the fruit he loved
drew a straight line in the sand around a curve,
spoke of ways, roads, lines of thought that converge
but never meet, and remember,

said the Spanish traveler, if you wallow in your wonder,
the thunder of those guided by imagination will be upon
you in a second, for you have what should be guarded
on this most dangerous planet for every waken moment,
you must follow the pathway of your lines, climb the jags
of far rock, take thine heart above the foam,
hear at once what the sea has said about finding home,
and how making something new means you must forget.

Never could I forget the fury of a sudden sea spout,
seen afar from where we sat, then upon us, its wind
took my cigarette–as ghostly Maimon rose and said,
of the marvel *Imagination:* how it sprouts with the *Intellect.*

URI

In the land of milk and honey
the legless soldier, drunk and angry,
gunned his Buick up to the Heights.
Driving like he was on patrol,
sticky hands on hand controls,
before dawn through Jericho,
the old world looked very old,
the old world on a moonless night,
nothing in the holy land
but two poorly aimed headlights.

DEAD VLEI IN THE RAIN

(with Lloyd Camp)

Rained on in Dead Vlei, when the sand dune
turned wet red, the blue sky turned dead tree,
and the dead tree stood—quiet in the quiet wood.

Dunes dry out, sit still, migrate slow,
horns downwind, carried by the river's whim,
to the sea, to the swell, to the beach to make a stand,
build a hill, sally forth and give up all for just the wind.

The wind will dry you out until you learn Dry.
It might not be that long a time. And when at last
you cut loose and cry, it will rain again in Dead Vlei.

THE OPEN WOUND

Young man with open wounds in the back of the bakkie,
wraps his arms against the wind, shivers like a springbok
before the Sun, knows cold rain, knows to wait, knows
fields of rust waiting in the wind, in the wind falling
like machetes in the shadows of threads torn away,
where children learn to say, yes sir! hell yes!
They march away and the sky goes blind.

The gouged eye of the Sun no longer shines.
Rivers run red from brown, finger-like clouds fall down

to a mother on her knees, in the garden on the ground,
telling a warbler, he was a nice boy, but he came home
all gone. He came home down to boiled pap
in the afternoon, one-legged in the kitchen lounge,
fallen to conviction, listening to the rumble across the water,
shrinking from a lion with eyes of stone, screaming
across the desert night, kicking in the goddamned television.

I LOST IT

south of Solitaire, Namibia

I lost it on the road to solitude,
somewhere south of Solitaire.
I lost the urge to leave home.

This mud-cracked desert high,
this grand valley is enough,
there is nowhere else I want to be.

Now I can be
anywhere anytime and sometimes
I wake to find...

> walking a long hall
> trailing a small dog,
> pissing in cold rain,
> sniffing the dark,
> dark night, night
> of thunder and stars...

I no longer want to change the world.

Canyon rock. Hard
going down, down
by layer, down by grain,
down under thunder-named:
Kaibab, Toroweap, Coconino
Sandstone. Switching back
to shale, toenail turning
black, rock red and raw,
soft color and far - walking
down rattled, humping, high-
stepping, hurting at the knee,
bending to the wind, contouring
round, counting down the lines,
four-legging landslides—crumbling
and steep, down karst, down travertine.
Sipping Muav seep.
                Sundown at Supai
sunk down the Esplanade sky.
Red-walled allegiance vanished down
a blue carbon stream; satellites flare,
scorpions creep.
Rising to rock: towers, uplifts, buried
hogbacks, slumped blocks, exposed
folds—cracked and monoclined.
Flat-lined gaps of time—eroded wide,
raven-eyed, white-throated,
red-budded, big-horned, fossilized,
planetary yellow-bush hillside, slanting
from young Sun. Walking-Down-Man: out Tonto
legging long, thinking down, looking in, hiding out
in the shade. Raven gets a lizard. Century stalks
win, place, show, lay down, melt in the haze. Shade
on shade, buff on pink, green on gray, gray ridge on
a gray ridge day, fade and fade and fade away.
Down to a bright angel, down to black,
down to brown, down to still, unconforming,
uncaring slot of chasm time: dark, cold, polished
to glass stone, cooling slowly in. Black striped by white,
Vishnu shot by a burning dyke, crushing in, breaking down
to me now, lying on rock, taking its heat, dying slow by the river.

DANGER ON THE HORIZON

Kaname Harada, profile, NYT

Long-faced Mister Harada spoke
of killing perfect strangers. Men he knew
not by name but certain reflections

in canopy mirrors—what he saw
from the cockpit of his Zero
during the war…

terrified faces of those he killed,
drifting his plane going into the fight,
ditching his plane when the carrier sank,
defending his nation somehow
                  he survived

nightmares for forty years, living
with history stuck in his head
his country sworn to silence
born of long faced dread.

The 98 year-old former kamikaze
warned the youth of old terror,
and terror to come.

          And more than one child
on hearing of awful war in the sky
went dreamy-eyed, and dreamed of glory
to be gained in the coming fight.

THIS GUY FROM THE SKY

for Matthew Bennett

When leaves cover the octopus and rocks fall from the sky,
I see my head as a rock, don't ask me why
I am a piece of the fallen sky.

THE CROSS-EYED POET-SCIENTIST

The cross-eyed poet-scientist, as a child, always forgot
where he had just been, so he had to relearn
every place, every name, the name of the day,
how to sit down, and for what the knife
and fork are used. He used building blocks
that he saw tumbling in the dark, coming to rest,
revealing answers and elements fitting together.
Pondering the bonds of thing and thought,
tracking the shadows of wild dogs, leaving
nothing silently behind, but his words
that fell into lines that defined his nights and days,
recognized, fine, and flipped astray.

JUST LIKE A PTERODACTYL

When the moon sails over the clouds over the sea
I sing out loud, my oh my how the rocks have changed,
the long lines of them, the seawall pointing down the island
of sand, linear with the mainland, undulating in the ways of sand
caught in the throes of a shallow sea,
shifting on its own time, right on time
meek rollers roll, persistent lines of them,
building, curling, breaking, and disappearing
over my shoulder a pelican dives into the water.

OH MAN!

I, modern man,
left the forest for the plain,
but I miss the trees,
and feel hugely estranged.

JERUSALEM VIA DOLOROSA

on a rooftop with Mohammed

He poured sweet wine from a flagon,
took my queen with his pawn.

High over the walled-in town, French
troops passed some Lebanese around.

Pilgrims in the street carried the Christ
and sepulchered up to Calvary Hill.

We sailed paper airplanes, someone sang,
'…Save the sinner, cut Him down…'

Easter came with the British twits
who spread their dunce and missed
the point.

A point appeared in the eastern sky.
Another dark cloud. Assyrian eyes.

Midnight prayers disturbed the air.
We paid our debts to the minarets.

The chess board was set aside.
Everyone was as if among friends.

Everyone has nothing but friends
until the hour comes and the ceasefire ends.

CRACKS

for Hollis

Between signing the agreement—and implementation
stands a gulf where persistence reigns. In a dry land
awash in weapons, things work best
when the day only listens, when someone learns

something new: capabilities, edges, languages, new forms
of perseverance arise, even then, cracks form, even when
the Sun shines only three hours a day in late Spring,
weeds peek, climb, suck vague moisture, move minute
nourishment through peristaltic pressures that, squeezing
for light, widen cracks in sidewalks, and life. Cracks

cracked by a fibrous yearning and racing against
                    Summer's descending clock;
green shoots break apart hard rock: Persistence
is a helpless choice; first comes water, then comes ice.

LEONID METEOR SHOWER

for Camron

Three in the morning Simon's singing alarmed
me back to forays in the 70's—in mountains,
hiking and climbing the Sisters, North Cascades,
Bitterroots, Bighorns, the Tower, the Valley, Josh,
and all those trips downriver. Lying in bed I held on
to something forever long gone.

Got up, went out back with blankets and Cam,
watching specks of dust formed with the Sun,
shed from a comet, crossing by chance, earth's orbit,
gaining friction, burning thrilling streaking across the sky,
leading to the thought: even if nothing is ever entirely lost
or won, it's okay for some things to be forever gone.

FAMOUS METEORS OF THE EARLY 21ST CENTURY

for Vanyon and the Fine Doctor

Dull-minded from all the 'harm done'
(in the name of a greater 'good')
I lay sickened, weakened, waiting
for more - with no energy to read anything
but the sports page, or Dante. Demons
of victory and angels of defeat appear together
where each measures each, and the planet spins.
On the TV a ball game begins.

Between the lines is international intrigue,
muscle and détente, feigning and bowling
over the weaker managers (of self.) Tobacco
stains on a refugee, invited for something to believe,
up to the Bigs in early Spring—
        when Leo ascends and the planet spins.

At 4th and long the game begins. Unsure,
Mr. President pulls the plug, unleashes a force,
reconsiders and calls it back, pulls, unleashes
and calls again, like the pitcher who pitched too long,
his arm one day just gave up and went
around the planet, spinning, spinning, spun.

The weak go down to the hyena. The Un-Eaten
puff at their good fortune and relax, gathering.
The fortunate build their forts and break down
bonds, beat the odds, or the wife, or the son,
or the Sun, and repent, all the while the planet spins.

The high Priest forgives,
spreads his arms over one of his flock stricken down.
An assistant prepares an IV and jabs it in my arm.
In the face of the Priest I see, as I fall fast asleep,
all of western medicinal history.
Venus slides to the west. Venus slides to the east.
A poet is born. The planet spins. A poet is born

under an auspicious star. Laboriously, he turns
to the Sports, where teams rise and fall in the C suites.
Business is intrigue, muscle and détente.
Fortune depends on a certain tendon, a tendency
for the predator to be most honest—drawn into
that dead-gaze. Neck first or any orifice,
the easiest way in is the most honest. The planet spins.
The Sun shines. On a warming globe in winter
the patient on the gurney sits up and sees…

the shelves are full of other selves.

In the time of the drone the TV is on,
the Big Game, long ago begun,
when the planet spun, and so did Venus,
the Moon spins too, just look at its face:
rabbit-eyed and vigilant over the planet circling.

A young southpaw fires a fastball, high and inside,
the batter leans into the planet's spin, whacks a fly.
It's a foul, a long strike. Guy in the cheap seats dives,
makes the catch, stands up bleeding, arms waving,
visage displayed on the scoreboard screen.
On a rock hurtling through the enormous sky
everyone becomes suddenly famous.

METEORITE

for Dave Mason

The man of stone
said the mud will return.
The rock in his hand
heard nothing of the man,
its tone was much too slow,
it cared not for the skin
in which it was held
at the bottom of its fall,
found by the man where it fell,
the man who knew no walls.

THE HORSE TOOTH

With Ty in the hills northeast of Cheyenne,
I found a horse tooth in the Oligocene
White River Formation. I gave the fossil
to him and talked about evolution

of the horse—who lived here
35 million years ago. "Then,"
I said, "it was warmer. Imagine,
Wyoming was tropical!" He was silent.

"You're a lot bigger than that horse."
I went on, "The older a horse tooth,
the smaller the horse - until Eohippus,
the first horse, 50 million years ago. Imagine,

a horse the size of Jack the Dog!"
Ty finally looked up and asked,
"Will there be a swimming pool
at our hotel tonight?"

CRAZY MARY THE MINER

She's a miner of dawn at the base of the rock,
in the heart of the flood she ticks what clocks,
runs with the wild scientist in frocks,
reminds the child of the lunatic fringe.

She cringes a hungry boy, fatherless, lonely,
slant hallway empty, thin limbs gone awry.
Wraith-like she hovers over aspens that quake,
longs for one thing that will never shake.

Mary haunts edges where workers wager
self-worth versus badges of loss-mounted pleasure.
Inhaling, she sexes, so easily bored
at lovers' correctness, she prefers girls
and men who crave what they can not handle,
gives a rusty shave, leaves 'em hung on a spindle.

She stimulates conflict in the mind of the frend,
fondles her edicts, lines up with the dead.
Stirring thin wine broth, drying a wolf liver,
she buries the cloth of a desert-light loner.

Crazy Mary needs not food to feed, she's a miner
of what is underneath. She digs and digs
and she believes in digging what cannot be seen.

LIVES OF THE POETS

There were mountains climbed in the mist
and the mist, as it must, grew thick with rime.
Up from the cave came a darker art, for art's sake?
For god's sake no one said it would be easy.
It left us wary and grappling with many
sad songs, until at last the lost face,
lost in lines, found some *-so what-* to say,
okay.

For all things familial it is far from abnormal
to be knocked out of orbit yet helplessly remain,
like a rubber band stretching, open to snapping
back to some kind of normal node.
There are mountains and mountains
erode.

FIVE

COFFEE AND CLOUDS

the fired mind with a smoke
in green planted window nook
out the early upstairs cloud
by the window soft me now

blue cloud high wind blown seed
through what eye do I perceive
sit quiet yellow bird now fly
clouds drift the horsehead sky

burned green to red to brown
hung naked above the ground
held up to the all-fall-down
dead tree stands glory bound

white cloud blue hard at six
nature lovers play god tricks
sit quiet last leaf blow free
clouds drift unknown schemes

room to room the mind will bend
coffee black with a dead friend
in the miracle of just another day
things you said I heard again

blue cloud no more red wine
only green now is the pine
sit quiet in space what for
clouds drift, want no more

FLEW OFF AN EAGLE

Turning west on the way to 16,
the Book Cliffs loom above the soft dried sea.
The Cretaceous beach, now slowly receding
tough rock, loses to the sun in a redverb spasm.

Two ravens squawk, float tiny over a knife-ridge:
slope and cliff, mud and sand, sea rise and fall,
wave-like the beach came and went, back, back,
back and forth.

On layers of sandstone and shale, I walked
with the small dog, oblivious to scale, coyotes yipped
their yip, I found an eagle feather and thought,
I could almost believe in god.

Even I walk on water - several months a year.
Up high, unseen movement heard loud…
rock fall echo down and recede from the coal-
ladened ridge, the snow-covered valley looks Paleocene:

One or two dim lights, then three.
Quick tongue primates build shelter,
kindle fire and gather together.
Humanity on the edge of the sea.

Young Venus, sharp above the western dune.
To have one true friend in this life is enough.
Twice last week on the ridgeline, a coyote
leapt into the sky and flew off an eagle.

THE STENCH

The colossal animal lay still, arrested against a low sand hill,
like an abandoned couch left to rot out on the plain.

They drove in closer to an awful stench; the elephant
was dead. On its bloated back a boy curled in a crude bed.
Who is this boy? they all thought. One asked, is he hurt?
is he lost? where's his home? what can we do?
where shall we turn?   The stench

seemed only to grow, when all at once they knew
           what they did not want to know,
there was nowhere to run, like any animal
they stood there dumb, looking down
the barrel of the rising man's gun.

ISOSTACY

> *If human is the goal of the divine creative will,*
> *what is this ringing in my ear?*

It warmed and the ice retreated. Rid of the weight
the province rebounded. A quick bloom of tribes
spread from the mouth of the Vistula: at Thörns,
Elbing, Königsberg, Dantzic, the banks of the Oder,
and the sea coast of Meklen and Pomer.

They made a mead to soothe the soul.
They made religion to suit the sun.
They swelled and played, plundered and craved.
They rode up the reindeer way. They rode cold east
with some idea of a rising warmth.
They sailed horses to the western islands.

> *…the spreading masses knew to farm, fight, and find*
> *better metals to harden mystic hammers, and swords*
> *to plunge the enemy wet like geology the ground went red…*

They learned to love as love was learned—
from something snugged and enveloped.
The beast within found ways to keep the beast within,
and still, Leviathan remained close.

Terror for terror to keep terror hidden below what rises
when fears excite us when swords duel when old doubts
when hard times flare up—within comes out,
makes a big mess.

Along the old highway—
upright walkers make their way, again, turning
from a newly risen bay, they drive, most civilized,
up smooth inland blacktop, up to the old Piedmont,
where gardens have grown stronger these recent years.

IT WAS VERY STRIKING

At the anti-war rally one of the peace protesters
got into a fight in the middle of the street, caught
no doubt, on film, by the cops across the walk.
An intentional knuckle caught the thought:
even the war here can't be stopped!

The weight of that turned to the long line of this
animal walking with uncertainty, balancing on two feet,
living in close proximity, attempting grace in the big dark,
chatting, chirping, driving, texting, waving to one another,
wave to wave to one another way to look at it…now and then:
clarity

strikes.
We broke up the fight with a bit of fighting,
hunching, feigning, adjusting caps, everyone
nodding and falling back to *their own* side.

CHRISTMAS READING

The geese are flying and I am reading
Matthew, imagining being spoken to
straight from the mouth of God.
Heard through a hole in a cloud?
On an otherwise normal day?

Would the beasts and birds pay
attention at all? Would I grow
weak in the knees? Yes. I would
fall, helplessly, upon encountering
God. In a manger at sunset?

In a desert hamlet? Yes,
it would be a pastoral scene—cows lowing,
goose bumps, God, and me, standing in a field,
an average Joe, kneeling before God.
That would rock my world!

I'd up and dance in a circle, kick up my heels,
move my family to Egypt. I would listen
close to the words of God, how I would,
would they only appear. Alas, I remain

in a world of stone, with fine green trees
acknowledging the prevailing winds.
I fall only for the day, everyday,
and pray to the ridge across the valley,
framed against the hot blood sky.

THE RAPTURE

Rapt? Sure!

GENGHIS KHAN ON A MORNING LIKE THIS

Silver trees in early sun, blackbirds call
all tortured souls, white doves call
all is well, captives line along the wall.
Heads fall.   Birds of prey

in a circle sky, clumps of clay
and a marching band, on the road
transformation is talking to a toad.
Kiss me now oh bloody word.

EK BALAM

Under
the heavy
air and light
from the bright
star of the jaguar they
tried to get a grip every
day with the whip of the long
sun. Fingers on sharp rock one
by one. Rocks pile high. Pyramid
rubs the sky. My uncle, my brother,
and I become intimate with the moon,
learn to value no thing, learn to build some
thing from zero with roads in every direction. Up
stone steps you climb to a darkening sky with crossed
sticks to touch god falling in the west. Your arms hold up
the sky but the clouds break down your brown legs. Water
rising. Still you stand, all through the night, needing to tell some
thing to someone. Needing to find the time. Needing to get a grip on
the tree in the thick of the green you cling to this rock under the sun. You
cling to this crust with your new slant your new thrust; the look in your endless
eyes. The trees bend under all your questions. The diving man dives, the serpent god
ascends, the pyramid turns gold. The sky watcher stares into the rising sun pleading
for more light.

COUNTER CURRENTS

What lies on the counter does not lie,
does not say a word, speaks volumes…

The edge of an indurated ash spear point says,
100,000 years ago some man sat here flaking,
grunting, bleeding, thinking, looking at the stars.

An iron cast of an iron ball in a lunar-like crater
but younger cretaceous only a place
for the thumb to thumb.

Rhombohedral calcite crystal, rhombohedrally needs to be
picked up, felt about with fingertips, looked at
clear through, cloudy, angled, morphed and helpless
(I could have been an evaporite without a tongue!)

A polished chunk of Nama Dolomite fits ripe
in the palm, a coral brain, formerly sentient rock?
sandblasted a million years, can no longer talk.

Slow thought: shark tooth—great white
from Carolina's phosphate, dug up by the dozer load.
Dangerous sea. Scream. Munch.

Professor in a white suit in full moonlight
sold me the fallen meteorite,
that sits on a trilobite from older hills, ("in that country,"
'ol Spit Chin said, "you can be your own granddad.")
("when I first got that rock I slept with it")
Jesus is the name of the trilobite.

Rising from that space rock, a magnet tower
from the toy store, where the Toy Store Guy
stood behind a display of force at a distance
that made my head ice cream and leap with joy
like a circus porpoise, like the tautness of air
pushing nothing but air pushing on the counter
one magnet against another - is magic – to think
of pieces of air and the spaces between the pieces.
(at the super bowl party I dropped the pizzas.)

A bowl turned by Old Sir John-On-The-Lathe,
(died 1945?) Everyone spins his tops, like magnets
they attract thoughts of places that speak
to the possibilities of balance on a planet spinning,
slowly slowing down, begun to wobble—
and so reveal: The Reasons for the Seasons.

The Fall will come, that's for sure, it always does,
for wobblers wobbling everywhere a bit too far,
off the counter through the floor, all the way in
to the center of a star – Fall In >< Fall Out – mind
goes supernova: the heat of molecular feeling felt,
falling, thinking, knowing what's going down.

Nothing then but a sandy beach,
a pier you take evenings for drinks, (down below,
small cilia undulate in pulsing waters) you think
to attach synthetic barnacles to the pylons.
Spin, spin, spin, and so, Monkey Man learns
to harness the Energy of Ocean Currents!

THE FIRST STONE

Going far, the human thought, farther,
so took another, saw in the mirror a shroud
fall from an ape face--etched with restraint.
With sticks the first symbol was scratched:

dark marks on stone, footprints in gray,
blink thoughts writ down, reflex storms
in the brain, sparks in the folded gray, folded
where time passes slowly away—like the wind

on the warm skin of early night, when the gray
is oh so bright, when a folded thing way out in space
sounds like the unheard sounds that sound...
when the full moon strikes upon the ground.

ACKNOWLEDGEMENTS

Thanks to the following publications where some of these poems
previously appeared:

*The Nervous Breakdown, Malpais Review, Santa Fe Literary Review,
Pilgrimage, Fruita Pulp, Grand Junction Daily Sentinel, Mountain Gazette,
Comstock Review, Illuminations Literary Journal, Prospective: A Journal of
Speculation, A Democracy of Poets, San Pedro River Review, Grand Valley
Magazine, plantsandrocks.blogspotcom, Ghosts of Giant Kudu, Pinyon,
Sage Green Journal, Fungi Magazine, The Telluride Watch.*

Thank you Jim Tipton, Jack Mueller, Wendy Videlock, Art Goodtimes,
Rosemerry Wahtola Trommer for your encouragement, intensity, and
devotion to language. Thanks to Kyle Harvey, Jen Hancock, Juan Morales,
Sandra Dorr, Frank H. Coons and the widening Lithosphere. Thanks to my
sista Sue for listening all these years. Thank you Vanessa for your vibrant
way, your fired mind, and for all the possibilities.

Danny Rosen founded Lithic Press in 2008, and the Lithic Bookstore & Gallery in 2015. This is his first full length collection of poems. His second chapbook, *Ghosts of Giant Kudu*, came out in 2013 from Kattywompus Press. Danny's genetically based optimism is steeped in his familiarity with deep time and big space. He studied geology, astronomy, and science education at University of Wyoming and Harvard. For many years he ran the Western Sky Planetarium, providing astronomy education for schools and communities throughout western Colorado.